Hats Off to You

A Celebration of Women

Compiled by
P A M   F A R R E L

Paintings by
S A N D Y   L Y N A M   C L O U G H

HARVEST HOUSE PUBLISHERS
Eugene, Oregon

Hats Off to You

Copyright © 1999 Harvest House Publishers
Eugene, Oregon 97402

Library of Congress Cataloging-in-Publication Data
    Hats off to you / compiled by Pam Farrel ; paintings by Sandy Lynam Clough.
        p.   cm.
    ISBN 1-56507-904-3 (alk. paper)
    1. Women—Quotations.   2. Quotations English   I. Farrel, Pam. 1959-
    PN6081.5.H38   1999
    082'.082—dc21   98-41742
                                                                              CIP

All works of art reproduced in this book are copyrighted by Sandy Lynam Clough and may not be reproduced without the artist's permission. For information regarding art prints featured in this book, please contact:

Sandy Clough Studios · 25 Trail Road · Marietta, GA 30064 · (800) 447-8409

For information regarding other books by Pam Farrel or her speaking schedule, please contact:

Pam Farrel · 629 S. Rancho Santa Fe #306 · San Marcos, CA 92069 · (760) 727-9122

Design and production by Garborg Design Works, Minneapolis, Minnesota

The author and Harvest House Publishers have made every effort to trace the ownership of all poems and quotes. In the event of a question arising from the use of any poem or quote, we regret any error made and will be pleased to make the necessary correction in future editions of this book.

Scripture quotations are from the Holy Bible, New International Version Copyright © 1973, 1978, 1984 by the International Bible Society. Used by permission of Zondervan Publishing House; the New American Standard Bible, © 1960, 1962, 1963, 1968, 1971, 1972, 1973, 1975, 1977 by the Lockman Foundation. Used by permission.

Printed in China.

99 00 01 02 03 04 05 06 07 08 / PP / 10 9 8 7 6 5 4 3

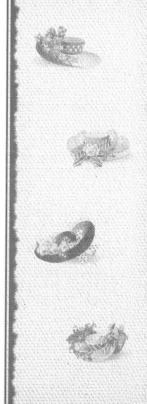

Hats Off to You!

Hats are worn for special occasions, like weddings and Easter. They are tipped in honor, waved overhead in excitement, and flung wildly in the air in the thrill of accomplishment. Hats represent the unique, wonderfully special times of life. The hats on these pages are tipped in honor of you, the person you are, the person you've become. You're a success in the eyes of all who know you. You're loved and appreciated, not just for your accomplishments but even more for the character of your soul.

HATS OFF!

You're a Woman of Priorities!

Priorities create the time to reach for the stars while you are reaching into hearts. Knowing what to do, and when to do it, is the key to success. Priorities reveal your true self. They are like a reminder string around your heart, gently pushing you toward the important tasks and people of your life. In the end, it will be your priorities that make up your eulogy, and your priorities will be engraved on the hearts of those precious people crying at the graveside. Priorities carve your place in this world one heart at a time. Most importantly, priorities keep your heart focused every day, every moment you are alive. Priorities are the stepping stones to your dreams.

Balanced women never get anything done, focused women do!

ANNE GRAHAM LOTZ

It is not easy

to find happiness in ourselves

and it is not possible

to find it elsewhere.

AGNES REPPLIER

Do first what only you can do.

DAISY HEPBURN

"Who knows but that
you have come to royal position
for such a time as this?"

An uncle to his niece, Queen Esther, who risked her life for a nation and won

THE BOOK OF ESTHER

At the end of your life you will never regret not having passed one more test, not winning one more verdict, or not closing one more deal. You will regret time not spent with a husband, a child, or a parent.

BARBARA BUSH

It's better to have a rich soul than to be rich.

OLGA KORBUT

Above all else, guard your heart,
for it is the wellspring of life.

THE BOOK OF PROVERBS

Goals are just dreams with deadlines.

EMILIE BARNES

Life is a coin. You can spend it anyway you wish,
but you can spend it only once.

LILLIAN DICKSON

She has achieved success who has lived well; laughed often and loved much; . . .who has filled her niche and accomplished her task; . . .who has always looked for the best in others and given the best she had; whose life was an inspiration.

MRS. A.J. STANLEY

Blessed are the flexible
for they shall not be broken.

AUTHOR UNKNOWN

To be successful, the first thing
to do is fall in love with your work.

MARY LAURETTA

13

HATS OFF!

You're a Woman of Excellence!

Excellence is the beaming smile of an Olympian standing on the winner's dais with a gold medal for a necklace. And the pursuit of real excellence can build a personal winner's circle. Excellence makes you feel like a winner, and it makes others see you as a winner. Excellence earns respect, admiration, and opportunity. Excellence isn't just an exterior standard but an interior motivation to do all things well. Excellence reveals character. Character builds trust. Trust creates hope. Hope yields a future. Excellence matters.

Do what you do better than anyone else that is doing it and you'll always be a success.

FLORENCE LITTAUER

Opportunities are usually disguised as hard work,
so most people don't recognize them.

ANN LANDERS

Being powerful is like being a lady. If you have to tell people you are, you aren't.

MARGARET THATCHER

Getting to the top isn't bad,

and it is probably best done

as an afterthought.

ANNE WILSON SCHAEF

What you are is God's
gift to you. What you can
become is your gift to Him.

HENRIETTA MEARS

*Opportunities correspond
with almost mathematical
accuracy to the ability
to use them.*

LILIAN WHITING

*There are two ways
of spreading light:
to be the candle or
the mirror that reflects it.*

EDITH WHARTON

Success can make you go one of two ways. It can make you a prima dona—or it can smooth the edges, take away the insecurities, let the nice things come out.

BARBARA WALTERS

Many women do
noble things, but
you surpass
them all.

THE BOOK
OF PROVERBS

23

It's not how many years we live but what we do with them.

EVANGELINE BOOTH

How we leave the world is more important than how we enter it.

JANETTE OKE

The secret of joy in work is

contained in one word—

excellence

To know how to do something

well is to enjoy it.

PEARL BUCK

Each one of us is God's special work of art.
Through us, he teaches and inspires, delights and
encourages, informs and uplifts all those who view our lives.

JONI EARECKSON TADA

It's not enough to be good if you have the ability to be better.

It is not enough to be very good if you have the ability to be great.

ALBERTA LEE COX
GRADE 8

You have to accept whatever comes, and the only important thing is that you meet it with the best you have to give.

ELEANOR ROOSEVELT

Our deeds determine us as much as we determine our deeds.

GEORGE ELIOT

Influence is earning the right
to be heard in another person's life,
for their good and for their benefit.

PAM FARREL

Whatever is true, whatever is honorable,
whatever is right, whatever is pure, whatever
is lovely, whatever is of good repute, if there is
any excellence and if anything worthy of
praise, let your mind dwell on these things…

THE BOOK OF PHILIPPIANS

You're a Woman of Vision!

Vision sees a path when there is none. For more than forty years, one woman believed that all of America would be better off if women could vote. Some laughed at her, others tried to ignore her, still others threw her in jail. But Susan B. Anthony had a dream. She could see a brighter world, and her words implanted a vision in other hearts. Fourteen years after her death, the Nineteenth Amendment was signed, and women gained the right to vote. Vision is a single candle lit on a dark night. One spark ignites in another heart, then another, then another—light added to light until dark is diminished. Vision is the ability to see with the heart what no one can see with the eyes.

You pay God a compliment by asking great things of Him.

SAINT TERESA OF AVILA

Not knowing when the dawn
will come, I open every door.

EMILY DICKINSON

God and one are a majority.

MARY SLESSOR

I have held many things in my hands and lost them all; but the things I have placed in God's hands, those I always possess.

EARLINE STEELBURG

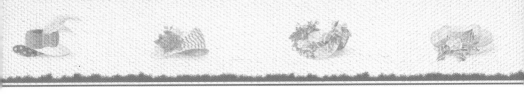

*How wonderful it is that
nobody need wait a single moment
before starting to improve the world.*

ANNE FRANK

*Optimism is the faith
that leads to achievement.
Nothing can be done
without hope.*

HELEN KELLER

Vision plus hard work equals achievement.

PAM FARREL

You may be disappointed if you fail,
but you are doomed if you don't try.

BEVERLY SILLS

If you are unhappy
with your lot in life,
build a service station on it.

Forgetting what lies behind and reaching forward
to what lies ahead, I press on toward the goal for the prize....

THE BOOK OF PHILIPPIANS

See each morning a world made anew, as if it were the
morning of the very first day; . . .treasure and use it as if
it were the final hour of the very last day.

FAY HARTZELL ARNOLD

If we had no winter;
the spring would not be so pleasant:
if we did not sometimes taste of adversity,
prosperity would not be so welcome.

ANNE BRADSTREET

Originality is not doing something no one else has done, but doing what has been done countless times with new life, new breath.

MARIE CHAPIAN

*The future belongs
to those who believe
in the beauty
of their dreams.*

ELEANOR ROOSEVELT

Do not follow where the path
may lead. Go instead where there
is no path and leave a trail.

MURIEL STRODE

*Always be a first-rate version
of yourself, instead of a
second-rate version of
somebody else.*

JUDY GARLAND

45

But risks must be taken, because the greatest hazard in life is to risk nothing. The person who risks nothing, does nothing, has nothing, is nothing. They may avoid suffering and sorrow, but they cannot learn, feel, change, grow, love, live. Chained by their attitudes they are slaves; they have forfeited their freedom. Only a person who risks is free.

ANONYMOUS CHICAGO TEACHER

Just don't give up trying to
do what you really want to do.
Where there is love and inspiration,
I don't think you can go wrong.

ELLA FITZGERALD

HATS OFF!

You're a Woman of Determination!

Determination is the heartbeat of a dream. Determination says success is sticking to the task when the feelings for it have disappeared. It's what ushers a dream into a reality. "Aerodynamically, the bumble bee shouldn't fly, but the bumble bee doesn't know it so it goes on flying anyway," says Mary Kay Ash. Determination keeps our wings flapping until what we hope for is ours.

Heat is required to forge anything.
Every great accomplishment is
the story of a flaming heart.

MARY LOU RETTON

She who hangs in the longest—wins!

PAM FARREL

When you cease to make a
contribution you begin to die.

ELEANOR ROOSEVELT

51

We must not, in trying to think about

how we can make a big difference,

ignore the small daily differences we can make

which, over time, add up to big differences

that we often cannot foresee.

MARIAN WRIGHT EDELMAN

Life is a succession of moments. To live each one is to succeed.

CORITA KENT

One can never creep when one feels an impulse to soar.

HELEN KELLER

To follow, without halt, one aim. There's the secret of success.

ANNA PAVLOVA

When you get into a tight place, and it seems you can't go on, hold on,
for that's just the place and time that the tide will turn.

HARRIET BEECHER STOWE

Run in such

a way

that you

may win.

THE BOOK OF
1 CORINTHIANS

*I do not know anyone who has
got to the top without hard work.
That's the recipe. It will not always get you to the top,
but it should get you pretty near.*

MARGARET THATCHER

God does not ask for ability or your
inability. He asks only for your availability.

MARY KAY ASH

When I stand before
God at the end of
my life, I would hope
that I would not have
a single bit of talent
left and could say, "I
used everything You
gave me."

ERMA BOMBECK

*A woman is like a tea bag—
only in hot water do you
realize how strong she is.*

NANCY REAGAN

People seldom see
the halting and painful step
by which the most significant
success is achieved.

ANNIE SULLIVAN

Success can only be
measured in terms of
distance traveled ....

MAVIS GALLANT

*I wish, I can,
I will—these are the three
trumpet notes to victory.*

ANONYMOUS

The only people who never fail are those who never try.

ILKA CHASE

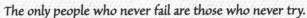

Success is never a destination—it's a journey.

SATENING SAINT MARIE

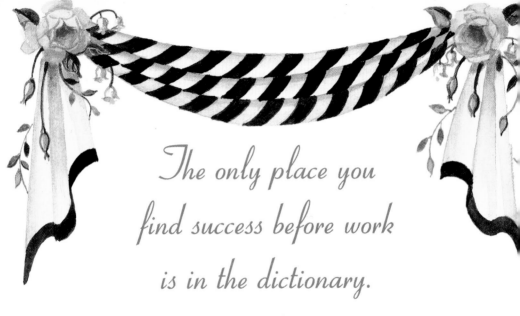

The only place you
find success before work
is in the dictionary.

MAY V. SMITH